They Are Almost Invisible

They Are Almost Invisible
Elizabeth Carmer

atmosphere press

Contents

This book is dedicated to Jessica, Lindsay, Barbara and Richard Carmer and their families for reading my individual poems before they were published.

Part I

A Wizard Can See Through the Woods

What is a wizard?
A person who will accept
you for who you are.
Against all stereotypical
odds, he or she
will not see
you as crazy even
if called that in town
one day.
You sought
out a wizard
personally
for this reason
and for reasoning.
Which you got.
Within a forest
visiting his/her home.
They made
you better
as a wizard
does
by calming
you and seeing
a different truth.
He/she thinks
you know more
than you know.
The wizard
is not personally
talking to you
they are knowing
that you are not

on the same page
as the accuser of you.
Wizards get caught
in attentiveness
not a lie. You walk
away knowing
the wizard is right
and you are wrong.
Your insecurity
did not endanger
the reputation
of that wizard
you saw.
It made
you turn around
in your steps
knowing
your enlightenment
is not yet
light years away.

A Wicked Half-Smile

The only witch hunt that I am familiar with is dealing with Salem,
MA. I went there in 2006 while working at a group home
in a different town. We saw the town around Halloween time.
It was not decorated nor were there crowds touring.
We understood that at the site of the witch trials. Where witches
were thrown into lakes to either drown or state the truth.
This treatment and trial is indifferent to human suffering. A trial
in a lake does not account for survival beforehand
and therefore is a slanted trial. To one side. A witch
may have felt she had a duty and right of her own and never
fled any scene. A female in a lake drowning is a modern-day curse
and plague of female brutality. There will always be that femme
fatale in the town who starts to lie and create an allegorical brush
fire against another girl. Innocent or not, the creator only saw dust
because she is actually from another terrain living in the same
town. Unfortunately, your law does not account for these
differences. And I doubt the reflection off the lake
showed the half-smile of the witch.

If You Dare to Drink

To sail is to know how to throw water overboard.
Whether you throw over starboard or port does not matter.
The main issue is getting water off the ship, the wood won't last
forever. While sailing, the crew may engage in drinking wine or
port. The water content of these is insignificant compared to
grape type. Drunkenness can ensue and what becomes of it?
Well what becomes of me or you when drunk?
Do you set sail, start to rhyme or find yourself
capsizing in intoxication? Are you fond of different types of things?
The build of a ship details a hierarchy; like the making
of a fine wine or port. Both of which are stored in wood barrels.
The sound a ship makes when approaching shore is low and
audible. The sounds within a winery are indeed from outsiders
visiting. The wood does not protect nor mask human voices; it
captures the essence of protection. When learning to sail, one
must be more diligent than when learning to take a drink. The first
time drunk cannot be the first time sailing too! Do you add water
to wine or port to muddle its intent, no. But water over due time
can help cure the ailments of being drunk.

The Tooth Fairy Was Obviously Female

The tooth fairy would give me a dollar a tooth.
The last dollar I remember receiving was given
coincidentally the weekend my godfather/uncle
Jamie was babysitting me and my two sisters.
They were older and I was the youngest.
I had never received formal instructions
of what to expect when I lost a tooth.
The morning of that morning, I woke up
without a bill. I told my uncle in the kitchen
and returned to my bedroom on the second floor.
Miraculously, my uncle came into my room
and slid his arm under my pillow, then left.
Did he leave without a trace? No.
A dollar bill was under my pillow.
Did I call my parents to tell on my uncle?
No, he was maybe trying to be a misplaced hero
for the tooth fairy. OK. I then offered
him the tooth that fell out. The details
as to whether I handed it over to my parents
when they returned are vague. I'm not angry.

Hello Kitty

We love you. We always have. Our daughters
wanted us to buy you and so you were bought.
You are the content of it's a small world after all.
You resemble the pleasantry of amusement parks.
Yeah, where families go or even Disneyland
Or Disneyworld where they vacation.
But wait, you are Asian? We believe in you.
You have that change purse, not focusing
On modern day wealth, but saving your money.
Hello Kitty is teaching us to wine and dine
Eventually. We can eat out like her in Japan
One day if we collect and then save our change.
She is our change. She is a girl in a girl's world.
Where is she sold? Every toy store? Unknown.
We support your quest to acknowledge adolescent
Females! You are so different than Barbie.
I don't feel used and abused when speaking
About Hello Kitty. You are merchandise that works.

Did You Run and Hide?

My favorite painting is "Guernica" by Picasso.
This piece does not represent a conspiracy theory.
I have actually seen it in the museum la Reina Sofia
in Madrid, Spain. I love the black-and-white features
which allow the muted grey to only represent
the significance of Nationalism. The conceptual
foundation of this painting is not grim. Its height
alone creates a vision of absolute truthfulness,
this painting really is that big. This painting is about anti-war cries.
I cannot quite identify this painting as anything but bravery.
The objectivity and directness show the severity of the dropping of
a bomb. These images show pain and struggle. This painting is not
to be ignored. This painting does not oblige others;
it overshadows the attempt to lie during a war.

We Have Never Seen an Ice Queen

An ice storm is not a grave for the entire world.
It is a demonstration of what is in the air. Frost
is a precursor to this event. It is on the continuum
of cold weather. A precursor is a dark cloud.
Icicles remain until melted, they seldom
are hit down with a shovel. They hang, creating
spectacles and not reflections to see.
They don't foresee the future. Ice falling
is dangerous but not inhumane. We can be warned
of its presence and to not drive. These weather
events are perhaps times to pray. But they don't kill you.

What About Her?

Was a corset a modern-day delivery of beauty?
This approach caught on worldwide mainly
for women. It accentuated the small waist
and curved bottom. The pushed-up chest
region apparently lost its importance
with this design. Its legality was not forsaken.
Desirability was only apprehended by wearers.
But its actual appearance was bland
and maybe underneath. Color was not integral.
Women even wore them to public hangings.
These were the more well-known women.
Robin Hood was a man of his word. He almost died
by hanging. Men of thieves relay the time
that these men pranced through woods
as swordsmen not delivering babies
as heroes but delivering riches to those born poor.
Was the English throne so deprived
as to mingle in the daily encounters
of woodsmen in the royal French countryside?
It has never been debated by women wearing corsets.

The Repetitive Sight of Seeing Only Sand

I spent a night in the Sahara Desert in Morocco.
I was lucky enough to have heard a parrot
repeating itself in a bazaar before departing.
Its image remains intact in my mind but its words
did not retain in my head. I was not hallucinating
in a guesthouse setting with provided hallucinogens
from Dutch tourists. I do remember being warned
and joked with by waitstaff, either Muslim
or not, asking if we wished alcohol while we dined.
We smiled and stuttered in French and Spanglish
even though not drunk nor getting drunk.
We were with tour guides who were Moroccans
and quite used to the journey. They had us engage
in a fake Moroccan wedding dance between sand
dunes. They spoke in Arabic in front of us and invited
us to their tent. We ate tagine but did not learn
how to prepare it, we were the guests. We saw
the sky clearly and its millions of stars, surprisingly
not wishing we were someplace else. Because we knew
this was only one night of our lives, we were not kidnapped
nor being taken against our will. I felt the worldwide
effects of terrorism and differences. But we did not try
to assimilate but did pay for henna applied to our hands.
The money was not applied to help a world war
or a developing nation, it was to show we were not victims
of war. Whether or not we knew that significance then.
The desert was not too hot to be unbearable.
The language barrier was not difficult.
We did not get married to the Moroccan tour guides.
We did not hide behind dunes too afraid of Muslim men.
We rode on camels and did not get injured.
We saw sand for more miles than we were used to.

An Artist Captured Her Smile

The jewel of the Nile is like the smile of "La Mona Lisa."
That type of painting created a rhythmic effect, called
oscuro, conflicting with what a nonbeliever thinks is heroism.
This non-jeweled effect allows the portrait to maintain
posture and therefore prosperity. She, the model,
is alive and powerful. Enlightening the general public
of what is good and bad. Did this curse against fake
elitists rupture towards Italy to destroy their art world too?
The Queen of Egypt does not come up when I search for her
on my internet OR any server. She rules like a God. Silently.
Did the theory behind oscuro create the Nile or its mystery?
Halfway between Islam is brotherhood and Christianity,
there lies the Gilded Age, Romanticism and artwork.
Men and women have always celebrated paintings
which they only hear about. Your heroism of seeing
something or anything reigns on.

A Glowing Moon is a Sight to See

A full moon does not destroy the earth to pieces.
Its creation is beyond us and its wonder is abysmal.
We only see it once a month. Waxing and waning
is the human proximity to death and God. But waxing
and waning go on uninterrupted, like us, until we die.
Where was the moon the day I did that? That is seldom
heard because we shun the moon and its wonder.
We pretend that the sun is better because the night
creates darkness when we are alive. An awakening
when we are only remains and witnesses that cannot
touch that planet. Its escape from us dictates mankind.
Its humaneness is an allegory for the man on the moon.
The North Star is brilliant and we can say that out loud.
The Big Dipper and Little Dipper are visible to us
and we assume their authority, like space cadets
during an air raid. We are separate and maybe unequal.

The Right to See

An eye exam is worldwide torture.
Or is it precaution and prevention?
I don't know because my lens
prescription changed at an increase
but I haven't filled it yet.
Before that, my longitudinal
understanding of these exams
was that they were punishment.
I was told in 2008 that I did not need
glasses. But I do. I need them to read.
But I sometimes trip and therefore
cannot wear glasses all the time.
To be completely honest, I forget
I have them. Their use for me is quite
cute, I do feel that people are taken
aback when I wear them, I must be smarter
than they thought. I have the prescription.

How to Not Destroy You

What is a tourniquet?
Is it sleep deprivation,
starvation
or pretending
to be someone
you are not?
Is it a bad
relationship?
It is maybe
swimming
when you can't swim.
It is lying.
When it is lying,
it is speaking.
It is then everything.
You feel cut off.
You destroy
all that you perceive.
You need nothing
allegedly
and you only
talk about yourself.

The Color of Death

When the Titanic did not make it to the NYC dock
did we automatically think that everyone died?
The Titanic was carrying people, it was an upscale
way to travel. Its descent was shocking.
Whose fault was that? The incident did not create
a world war between that continent and America, the sinking
of the Lusitania did. We can only ask how far
away was the iceberg when it was spotted?
We can only thank the movie *Titanic* for details.
The movie gave us an intimate look at its demise.
I tend to still ask how many women were rescued beforehand?
I also tend to focus on the fact that the lighting of the ship
did not immediately go off. Lights were maybe the last to go.
How scary it must have been to make contact with the ocean
water as a human being. That person was just on a ship
and is now lost at sea with an imminent death. To die
at sea is so nebulous. It's an unwritten truth that they died.
Was consciousness lost on behalf of the crew or guests first?
Lifeboats rescued but the distance to America was obsolete.

The Color of Freezing

The visual sight of an iceberg looks like broken glass.
It is not clear but sharp and rigid.
The Titanic unfortunately hit one of these ice pieces.
So detrimental was the hit, the ship collapsed and sank.

Victims froze to death out there in that ocean water.
How long was the wait to die? The sudden onset of shock
and subsequent fear are non-conditional symptoms.
When freezing and your heart collapses it is like

the scene where the blue diamond is thrown overboard.
"No, we just lost it!" The throw did not create a ripple effect.
Only a lifetime of memories in a lost scrapbook.
The descent of the diamond to the ocean floor is not poverty.

Part II

Grey is Neutral

What is your favorite color?
Mine is grey. I consider it a
shade of black and white.
Not to be translucent.
It represents uncertainty
and confusion. But logically
it is a reminder of hard fact.
Cement is grey.
Clouds can be greyish.
It is the in-between state
of light and darkness.

The Silhouette or Her or Me

What is a guidance counselor?
A remote person to assess you
or a real-life silhouette of
who I can become?

What We Hide

Pollution is a manmade catastrophe.
Its creation and progression collide
with natural wonder and beauty.

We attempt to hide what is thrown away.
This source of truth is actually a dump.
The Staten Island, NY, dump emits an odor.

That odor is toxic, like their accent. It is decayed waste.
Garbage itself is not regulated. It is lawful, obligatory.
Earth's understanding of human instinct.

We cannot omit that we are the creators of dumps.
Daily we hide behind the career of the garbageman.
His work is routine, without it we can't anticipate how to hide.

A Death of a Girl

She went by Missy and she died tragically.
She sat down by herself on the side of a road.
She was hit by a truck and probably died instantly.
Before she passed, I thought she would be a girl
to be a legend. She was so independent that she
could talk her way for miles. At such a young age,
her death was shared with the whole school.

What Seeing Nothing Can Make You Think

What is a ghost town?
Is it seeing a half-full hotel
or is it seeing an abandoned parking lot?

We tend to not imply disadvantage as ghostlike.
But if you were the victim of these circumstances,
you may tend to avoid these places referenced above.

Like the movie series *Ghostbusters* a library
or any library on a Saturday afternoon is pretty empty,
its environment could make one think ghosts exist.

Have You Ever

read the book *Go Ask Alice?*
I did in middle school. Does that make
me bad or a drug user (it was maybe recommended.)
No, I could just appreciate the bodily emotion

That was written about that girl. America
during that time was facing a crisis. Personal
catastrophe which that book represented, or jokingly
caught on tape, was instructive to youth in general.

I did not become a drug addict but I personally became
able to respond to difference. How? Well, I thought
that I should become more intelligent and if that was
impossible, I should become more knowledgeable

and not fake, like a false friend.

Oh My God

If my friend ever told me I was like Rayenne,
from that show *My So-Called Life*, I wouldn't
know what to do. She would be lying,
but I wouldn't tell her that.
No, I am not going to tell my parents.
Whoa, I just said "No" out loud.
Uh-oh did I just get caught talking to myself?
But she did that to me!
Wait a minute, that's not fair though.

You Can Never Forget the Law Like Your Name

A blank slate is not like a blank stare.
To reference the first clause, it is not
just schoolkid trauma from sixth grade.
It actually means nothingness.

We are sourced in actual processes.
We attain stability from legitimacy.
We cannot continue to believe that
the course of actual reality is solely verbal delivery.

Therefore, there is a means to an end.
We attained our names from a civil discourse.
We became and therefore are humane.
We tend to rely on humanity to state we are human.

The Meat Packing Industry

If you have ever walked through it, you might be reminded of Samantha from *Sex and the City*. Knowing very little about this part of Manhattan and having walked through it, I can say that I actually did see hanging meat carcasses outside. I don't feel that this part of the city is cut off, it is just different. The streets are by no means wider it just has different architecture. The overall demeanor of a warehouse is artistic, if you can learn to appreciate that sector of society. The glimpse into the warehouse is like a mind trap. You are in downtown Manhattan but know that a taxi ride up the West Side Highway costs at least thirty dollars as opposed to the subway. Would one change their diet and whole daily discourse if they saw meat hanging by becoming a vegetarian? I don't know. That might be more expensive of a lifestyle in the city. You can only know that the warehouse doesn't actually produce; it butchers and distributes. Whoa, this industry is markedly different than the fashion or modeling industry that you feel lost in if walking down that street at any time during the day. I personally know that I am not a model and have never been asked if I am a model. Am I offended? No. The movie and show *Sex and the City* reference the sex industry but that network feels less mainstream.

Picking Up the Check
at an Early Bird Special

30

To become an elder is like respect in every sensible way. To turn sixty-five warrants the federal government to turn you on to their benefits. You also then pick up on the delight and ultimate process of the early bird special. The specific advertisements that dinner begins at 5 p.m. is only appreciated for those it is intended for. Family members can accompany early birds to a restaurant. But don't pretend to be a witness to aging.

Do You Mind the Birds So Close to the Road?

Do you know that there is a bird sanctuary located in northern Massachusetts? That place is within Plum Island, closer to the ocean than Newburyport.   On the way to the most distant point

of the island, there is a dilapidated pink house. That house is now protected property with a sign stating to not cross, otherwise one will be prosecuted. The bird sanctuary is actually on the other

side of the road. The sanctuary certainly attracts visitors, more than flying birds. On a given day, a passerby can see professional photographers perched on the roadside with limited equipment

but silently shooting. Their equipment does not include a tripod. Therefore, the photographer is holding the camera and capturing birds seated themselves. The sanctuary offers protection

because it involves awareness and support of that species. It is not uncomfortable that Newburyport is allegedly a ritzy town and they live near where birds are protected. The land is actually beautiful

at any time during the day. The proximity to suburbia or city life is lost if you try to reach out and touch a bird. The open marsh expanse offers a whole new grid to a photographic memory in

America.

How Much is Too Much During "Therapy"?

I had just relocated home to New Hampshire to unfortunately live with my parents after a car accident. This car accident was not my fault and I ended up seeing a neuropsychologist who determined my IQ as having fallen nine points.
This neuropsychologist prepared a report, a typed report with an extensive history. But actually, I don't have a psychiatric history, only ADHD. And this person is not a prescriber of medication.
So I wanted to personally contest the hypothesized statements. This doctor stated that my car went over the curb and hit a tree at an MPH that I don't remember because I threw his medical notes away. I don't believe whatever he said. I purport that I went over the curb at a rate of 15 MPH and within about 50 feet I hit a tree head on at probably 8 MPH.
What happened? My airbag did not deploy but there was a crack on the windshield. It's just that I had a closed head injury (I learned that from him) with a visible bump on my upper left forehead. This bump was still present during my first voluntary appointment with this medical professional. He did not call the police nor question its presence, he insinuated my craziness. I had no hard evidence to deter his tactics and therefore did not know how to leave his office. He seemed inappropriate. I left the state of North Carolina and hoped to God that invalid report would not follow me home. I felt his demeanor questionable by law. I mean the guy administered me an MMPI— that is a lawful written exam. But, no one got those answers nor the overall conceptual progression of this man's growing anger that he actually wanted me to admit to being crazy and liking him more than I should? It actually turned out that this same person from New Jersey got his PhD where I got my undergraduate degree.

How I Responded to Him Gone

A bad breakup is like nothing you have ever experienced.
You wish you could state what he did that he broke my heart
and he is wrong.

But nobody is listening and allegedly nobody cares.
The worst of it is, all your current friends are his friends.
Therefore, we are done and there is nowhere to go.

I can watch movies and try to relate. But basically,
I don't want to see his happiness anywhere online.
His improvement is immoral and no one cares.

Canoeing is Not Intruding

Canoeing is done slow and shallow
in most cases. If you are lucky
you will have a scenic view
of vegetation, maybe lily pads.
Which you might stream through.
Your arm motion is reminiscent
of Canadian and American problems
when we were involved in the pursuit
of the unhappiness, overthrow
and demise of every tribe. In order
to overshadow their theories behind
how water ripples and affects the shore.
What creates a wave to an Indian?
When Indians were still called Indians
they might have been expert canoers.
They built their own and knew how to muddle
the wood after axing it down. The hollowness
of their canoes decries victory as their thought
process is visibly different than their over-throwers.
They may have not been doing what intruders thought.

When We See a Train Coming
While on the Track

35

The movie *Stand By Me* justified the concept of friendship.
We rely on the railroad track scene to discover what is real.
If we were on a track about to be hit, how would we save one?

We know we would because we already are on this journey.
We probably would run right away. That decision means
we are still friends. What comes next, whether it is good

or bad, cannot determine our future. The immediacy
of our previous actions allow us to feel good about ourselves.
We didn't wrong anyone right there, therefore we are right.

Part III

They are Almost Invisible

The wingspan of a hummingbird can actually attest
to human ignorance. The sound coming from the beating
of their wings is their actual ability to hover in midair.

The sugar content of their human-offered food source
tries to represent their bodily function. It is in no way
a lack of oxygen, their humming sound; this species is unique.

A Bumper Car is Your Joyride

Bumper cars are a joyride for who?
You who is bumping or me who is bumped?
I don't think whiplash is desirable
and therefore I am afraid of this activity.
You go, then stop, you stop then go.
You turn and get turned and want to know how
to fix it before the "ride" ends. When cruising
you dodge and get dodged in order to hit
that one bumper car. Whether or not you succeed
you must have made contact with the wall
which is more distracting than making contact
with a rubber bumper. Walking out of the ring
is laughing out loud. No one won and no one lost.

My Job Works for Right Now

To work in America is to make a living.
But the question is how much do you make?

People tend to lie about their income.
Because it is embarrassing to tell the truth.

Many people want others to believe
that they one day may have a pool.

What One Does After School

TV shows in America cost something to watch.
The money or meandering to pay for it are forgotten.
You either have cable or you don't.
No one has eradicated primetime TV
and therefore it is available to everyone.
Do people anticipate watching television?
This thought process is different
than attending school. It justifies feeling lost.

I Prefer the House Made of Seashells

Sea Island, GA, is part of the United States of America.
It is not an island but it juts out into the ocean.
In order to get there, you need to go through
St. Simons Island, GA. Marshes align the left coast.

The Cloister, in its heyday, was the island resort.
Slightly similar to the private golf club at the other end
of the island. All employees are randomly

or coincidentally African American. I don't feel
awkward, just aware. It is not uncomfortable
to say hi to the employees, it is just natural.

We actually stayed in a rental. The exterior
of the house was made of seashells.
After playing tennis my family and I would go to the Cloister.

It was like an upscale clubhouse. It was located at the beginning
of the island, like an entrance to your vacation. Alligators
were visible in the marshes, some randomly went astray.

I Knew I was Not an Olympian

Ice skating is a pastime of mine.
Where did I do this?
At the local pond that froze
over every winter.
This pond was called Beard Pond.
It was located across the street
from my middle school.
Trying to be better than you actually are
or better than you can be is dangerous.
The spike of the blade is sharp.
Trying to create picks in the ice
or designs while stopping
are not always successful.
I knew back then that trying to pull
off a jump was out of the question.
I would then become aware
that I had a one-piece snowsuit on.
That outfit was not representative
of Olympic skaters. I would try to not cry.

You Were Never Acknowledged as a School Bully

The middle ground between 100 and 75 is 88.
Why do I know that? Well, I received that grade
in fifth grade. Haha, not funny. I sat next to two
students who were not (considered by me)
as successful as me. I don't blame them
but I acknowledge their presence.
The grade was on a test which included an essay
and a multiple choice regarding weather systems.
Like clouds and precipitation. I didn't read into the test.
I don't absorb falsified knowledge. And I certainly
don't pretend and make up facts on an essay,
like my understanding of hues in a rainbow,
like that purple is a fake color. I am not destroyed
by my youth because these days I still keep in shape.
I look into myself as having not addressed my personality.
I was not elated to be a standard student, I was resigned
to the fact that I felt bullied but no teacher stated that out loud.

I Might Miss My Family While Driving

I drove from Boston to Syracuse, New York, today.
I actually departed from Roslindale and used
my GPS device. I had to take residential
side streets in order to make it to I-90.
Exiting Boston on this thruway is a straight shot.
The drive is comparable to any other five-hour drive.
Not long and no particular places to stop.
The gas station and accompanying eateries
provide the source for people-watching.
A hidden pastime of mine. Because this type
of symbolism is far different than the directional.
tour guide or tour book for tourist traps.
I feel noticed when I walk into a rest area.
Does that trap me? No, I just wish for a family of my own.

Tripping and Falling
or Being in Seventh Grade

47

I heard about a kid in my sister's grade who got burned in the face
while cooking fried eggs. I immediately thought the stove
must have been too hot. Uh-oh. Not later nor then did I think
he was high on drugs. He was in seventh grade. Did anything
ensue, no, he returned to school as normal without police issues.
It was like a real-life disclaimer, kind-of, as what happens
to your brain on drugs. That was a poster in restaurants
in the 1990s. I didn't want to think about that then.
Now, I am not professionally involved in that industry so I don't
apply these black-and-white statements to anyone. I am someone
who doesn't understand the message. Is it trying to destroy drug
use and its effects without disclosing potential physical injuries.
The injuries affiliated with drug use might be entirely different than
falling or tripping. My parents never had this sit-down dinnertime
conversation with us before, after or never.

How Close is Capitalism to Existentialism?

Ayn Rand was a writer who is maybe known to the average reader. Her approach to capitalism is a dialogue on an individual's existence within a market economy. Basically, how do you get to work? And more specifically, how close do you live to your job?

What an Issue Is

Onondaga Lake in Syracuse, NY, is so polluted that you cannot
swim in that lake. It is recommended to only eat one fish if caught
from that water source. But there is a refugee population in that
area who tend to catch more than one fish. This cohort of people
are from Burma. These people have high levels of mercury
and lead in their blood due to eating the fish. They fish
on the edge of the lake trying to be unnoticed. But they are
already here, so we must see them and know their whereabouts.
They have already been noted by someone, unfortunately not by
the whole world but by some governmental system. The census
does not pay tribute to their grievances but only for their numbers.
The public health concern is that these refugees did not know the
local warnings against catching and eating the fish. This aspect
deems them refugees. They still fish despite advisories maybe
because they don't see them. In all senses of irony, if the state or
local government put signs up on the side of the lake, would that
be futile? The refugees were not brought here to stand public trial
for causing the lake's pollution, that was created by a local
chemical warehouse. They came to seek safety. In their terms,
mercury levels and the salt density of a fish diet are non-issues.

The Local State Park is a Reminder that Some People Hike

A state park is in no way a dangerous place.
But it can be if you are not afraid to wander.
The average American may or may not access

such a place. And we can only hope they do.
Because honestly, we don't learn to hike in school.
We absorb guidance and therefore are educated.

To See Behind You While Hiking

Looking Glass Rock is located outside of Asheville, NC.
The slope and danger of the actual rock necessitate
such severe civility that you must not be a trespasser.
Your breathing air is not occupied nor destroyed up there.
You can see far distances but you are probably not looking
back at where you live if you reside locally. Your shoes
hopefully are still intact so you don't lose your balance.
Your thought process might be to hope your fellow climbers
are benevolent as a fall would be fatal. The hike up
can only weed out those who are not inclined to hike.

When We Got a Computer

Is it unreachable to get straight A's?
Am I a good student or a poor student?
Well of course I and other classmates know.
I read all assignments and attended all classes.
I gathered notes before and after school
in order to retain what I thought was taught.
I never excelled in school because I was busy
worrying about other things in general.
I played sports but never made it to varsity
early as overachievers tend to do.
I did play tennis but always felt that my game
was weak. It did not progressively improve
nor of course did not worsen.
I did not attend church during high school.
I was not in advanced classes but did
apply myself in order to get A- minuses
I only read Cliff's Notes once junior year.
We didn't get a computer until 1997—
therefore searching was obsolete.

That Car Accident

In the blink of an eye can things change.
They can and I know. I was in a car
accident in 2010—the car hit a tree

but only at 15 MPH.

How much did things change?
To dictate truthfully, quite a lot.
I had to resign from a new job.

As an unemployed person,
I then had to withstand
dictating to insurance

companies that I am owed money maybe?

Part IV

I Don't Go By Ann

My middle name is Ann
like every female
on my mom's
side of the family.
Is that tradition,
Italian
or trying
to maintain
a female name?

We don't spell
Ann with an e
at the end.
That escapes
us. We don't
talk weekly
on the phone
because of this
namesake.
But it is a nice
thing to remember.
Even if my two
same-aged cousins
are best friends
due to their proximity.
I do remember
when one
of their moms
told the two
of them
in front of me
that they will

be best friends.
But what about me?
I guess the middle
name similarity
is an example
of family.

Who made
this tradition?
I don't know.

The Social Ladder
Continues to Expose Itself

Now a totem pole is not something to climb.
If you did attempt to climb, after locating one,
what would transpire? Would this act/action
target Native Americans and their history?
Or is the perpetrator targeting USA law enforcement?
Either way in America, we need to associate truth.
We cannot continue to identify tribe as barbaric.
Some tend to climb the social ladder for mistaken causes.
Others use it as their education. But Native Americans
can try to remain calm and claim they were framed.

I Dare You

Have you ever dyed your hair black?
I have and not by mistake. This happened
during college. My friend
dyed my hair in our bathtub. During the rinse,
watching the dye run out was not like watching
a scary movie, it was me hoping this would work.
I thought that look would make
me prettier. Did it? I don't know. It eventually
lost its blackness and faded away but leaving
roots. The root cause of my insecurity
was something entirely different.
But the issue was that maybe falsified
intelligence could mask as gothic.
Like a stolen personality.

My Favorite Place to Go on a Walk

Green Lakes in New York is one of the greenest lakes you can imagine. This lake is so deep that it does not turn. Therefore, it is aqua-green. This color is so beautiful it is distracting. Not distracting to the point that you get lost while on the trail nor wander into the woods. The woods there are not too deep. The water is still. Murky water is more at the beach side where visitors swim during summer months. There has never been a missing-person incident, kidnapping or crime committed there. Therefore, it is serene and calming. The parking lot not threatening, this is a place for local visitors to relax. Why? This lake only permits proprietary rentals of kayaks, canoes and paddleboats. The excursion on the lake does not cause a natural disaster.

The trail around the lake is a breathtaking sight that is actually not in a world-renowned exotic destination. The lake also is next to an 18-hole golf course. My goal would be to do more picnic.

How to Belong After Learning Slang
While Living in Suburbia

When living in Spanish Harlem I did read that book.
While reading it, I did not have full electricity
nor air conditioning. I did have a full-time job
downtown (shhh in Soho). I did order takeout
and always paid in cash. I did not try to talk
in a fake NY accent. I thought if I left that out
I was more legitimate. I thought that rollerblading
along the West Side Highway park was ultimately
what made me independent. So much that I felt cool.
I didn't wear the clothes from the store where I worked.
I was being too influenced by that book. I recognized
that upbringing but never took it upon myself to visit
public housing by mistake. I continued to take public
transportation but got lost within that book.
I wondered the differences that existed between
me and you and you and her. My family versus you.
If that would ever be an issue. It wouldn't. My future
was based on whether or not I could graduate college.
I majored in Spanish to try to belong to a group
that I could not find in suburbia. Subsequently, I don't feel fluent.

How Far Away Is the White House?

The sound that motorcycles make is extreme during the summer.
I live in Portsmouth, NH, now and used to live in Rye, NH.
The motorcycles create a motorcade but I know this is not the
White House. This is only nearby to the road Route 1A that borders

the ocean. The couples on the bikes travel in packs like gangs.
They wear gear which sometimes has consistent features.
The revving of the engine is not directed at me while stopped at a
light. It is just them doing what they do. I am driving in a car when I

witness this. I am not a casual driver, I am a nervous driver. I would
feel shame if my music was playing so loudly that those outside
could hear it. I think that's illegal, like a noise violation or
something. This is New Hampshire, "Live Free or Die."

We are without taxes, not even property tax. Only tax on prepared
foods. But you don't have to legally go out to eat in order to pay
these taxes. In America, the state of NH deals with traffic
commerce. We sell alcohol non-taxed here. In state liquor stores.

Who goes there? Well, locals who drink, distributors, Mainers
and Massachusetts residents. I don't find these details unnerving
or dangerous. I just know that I have the personal right to not have
to ride a motorcycle. Thank God. I fear the helmet is not enough.

I prefer to state I am too scared to ride it.

How I Taught Myself Photography

I am a beginner photographer.
I tend to focus on urban landscapes.
The shadows, the lighting are attractive
to me and not necessarily mainstream
appeal. I like grunge. Why? My bedroom
was next to my oldest sister's—she listened
to Hole, Nirvana and Babes in Toyland daily.
I would walk to the pizza place where she worked.
She dated a skateboarder and she had an electric guitar.
I never took it upon myself to play air guitar nor break
into her room. She painted the walls black and the door gold.
I did not feel scared of her, she was artsy. My challenge
these days is learning to feel safe while practicing
to make a better photo.

Is a Piano Lesson Worth it in Sixth Grade?

The metronome device during a piano lesson is not an afflicted
head injury. It is a measure of time in order to make you the best
you can be for that recital. My mom and specifically my mom
is relying on me to excel publicly. But up until now, privately,
outside of school. My soliloquy is that if I do not make
this perfect, I might die. At the early stages of practicing,
I remember, do re mi, the repetition and the tune are familiar
and instructive. They are grounding. I am not grounded right now
while at my lesson because I am here. But my mom is pressuring
me to be better than everyone I know. This is not a school
activity and therefore my anxiety is unmanageable.

Student Body President Didn't Know

A perfect student turned out to be bad.
She lied all throughout high school
and all of us in her graduating class
found this out about seventeen years later.
Not at an alumni event or at a reunion.
No one saw this coming. She was student
body president. But she did actually go
to the local state university a lot now that I think about it
during senior year. She must have been partying there.
She is on the alumni association but fails to invite
multiple parties to events. She is self-focused
and not self-aware. It's too bad she spoke on behalf
of our private school and its endowment for so long
without intervention. She got away with a lot.
Did your dad do this for you and not to you?

What Wouldn't Make Me Blush

I had a made-up role, Foil 6, in the sixth-grade play.
I was not devastated but resigned to still move forward.
Would I still receive their makeup and costume?
I didn't know. But I continued to respond effectively
by attending Saturday morning rehearsals. I even attended
the actual first night. My role was as a caller who maybe
was trying to attempt to call the main female protagonist.
I did not consider this a personal attack at such a young age.
I considered it average accusation. I actually held the provided
cordless phone upside down during the first night. Whoops.
My parents, if they were there, did not stand up, walk out
or yell at me. I remembered my lines and recited them verbatim.
My role was completed and done. I didn't blush, it was the lighting
causing me to feel warm. I don't blush in general. For the record.

Where I Found You

was during a blades match.
You know, the act of fencing.
But an actual fight.
Your knife skills are different
and not as ambidextrous as mine.
Yeah, you, my rival.
You look intent and not scared.
You must have practiced
many times or many years.
Maybe you were an apprentice
who graduated with an elevated
skill and overthrew his teacher
not to kill him but to be his own master.
Your aim is discreet. You want to pierce
my heart but you are focused on my inner
body, not strength. Therefore, you are cheating.
The point of your blade is sharp which makes you think
you are on top of your game, alive, aware and unafraid.
But you trained in a closed game, an environment
which didn't make you think of outside objectives.
Your matches have only been with locals or contemporaries,
not enemies. Therefore you don't know what an enemy is.
You are you and not me. I notice you tend to favor
your right arm thinking that is power. Your strength
has never been tried and therefore you are unpracticed.
We are not actors but actual skilled people who are facing
one another. I don't know you but I know you think you rule me.
Your game is weak and I think you have played
more chess than this.

Family Graves Serve You

A burial plot is not female revenge.
This is an American family tradition
in order to provide for those
who gave us what we have today.

Can everyone in America afford
the same right? If you cannot afford
to be buried what do you do?
I think of Amadeus Mozart

and that movie recalling a public
burial plot. That mud hole
did not destroy what that man
had done with his life but showed

us the decisions made of those
impoverished during their life
and those made when they die.
That movie depicted a man

chasing a woman leading to his grave.

Does that always happen?

Think About That Deal Before You Go

What is a pawnshop?
It is not what you thought.
You feel uncomfortable there.
Probably about your income
and status. It's a place
where your stability is apparent.
You are there and therefore
want to buy. But you feel
muted almost. You want
to reference a broken record
but cannot because that would
be appropriate in a record store.
Down the street. Why are you here?
You thought you were getting
a deal from someone you knew.
But you're not. They left the item
to be bought. Your anxiety
is lacking legitimacy
to the point that you look suspicious
in this type of store. Maybe think otherwise.
Do still look both ways when crossing
the street but don't try to sell your soul.

The Crossing of the Alps

So, to cross the Alps is a task necessitating days
on end. But the von Trapp family did cross
and they founded the ski resort Stowe.

I personally consider this ski resort in Vermont
more than a tourist attraction. The movie
The Sound of Music is so meaningful and filled
with historical references that we seek to remember
that song, "Do-Re-Mi." As a piano player in America,
I was taught that song. The poetic connections
chose to alleviate the pressure of the war.

We all loved Julie Andrews who played Maria.
Her character was so vital to our understanding
of his (her lover's) actual persona during
the Holocaust, that this movie could be educational.

Anne Frank's Bedroom

Anne Frank was a girl who experienced hiding.
She is different than the average American girl
or a book character and its protagonist: this occurrence

was during the Nazi Invasion. Anne's personal
room was occupied only by her. To see it in Amsterdam
is difficult. She must have turned to reading or drawing.

Betrayal: the family lost their hiding spot given
a non-civil discourse, which led to exposure.
Anne is a protagonist here for being able

to overcome the monotony of fear daily
and for being able to write. Her diary appreciates
fear and the unexpected. We respect her father.

Tear Gas Makes You Think

Is the concept of tear gas different
than other policing techniques? I am not sure
because I am not used to this type of questioning.
Basically, I think that this process is an instance
where it was already determined that people need
to not be able to see. So, I guess this scenario occurs
during a riot to dismantle a force that has risen:
that force is opposition.

What is Law?

It is the monotony of the Constitution.
It is the obligation to examine and maybe
investigate. It is a legal and national
standard of living. We have laws
to try to maintain stability. We have lawyers
to interject verbally. We have judges
to counteract arguments. But we have a jury
made up of the general public.
Jury duty allows people to see, hear
and understand each side. We wouldn't
know any other process.

About Atmosphere Press

Atmosphere Press is an independent full-service publisher for books in genres ranging from non-fiction to fiction to poetry, with a special emphasis on being an author-friendly approach to the challenges of getting a book into the world. Learn more about what we do at atmospherepress.com.

We encourage you to check out some of Atmosphere's latest releases, which are available at the press website, Amazon.com, BarnesandNoble.com, and via order from your local bookstore:

Transcendence, poems and images by Vincent Bahar Towliat
Adrift, poems by Kristy Peloquin
Time Do Not Stop, poems by William Guest
Bello the Cello, a picture book by Dennis Mathew
Let the Little Birds Sing, a novel by Sandra Fox Murphy
Ghost Sentence, poems by Mary Flanagan
That Scarlett Bacon, a picture book by Mark Johnson
Such a Nice Girl, a novel by Carol St. John
Makani and the Tiki Mikis, a picture book by Kosta Gregory
What Outlives Us, poems by Larry Levy
How Not to Sell, nonfiction by Rashad Daoudi
That Beautiful Season, a novel by Sandra Fox Murphy
What I Cannot Abandon, poems by William Guest
All the Dead Are Holy, poems by Larry Levy
Rescripting the Workplace, nonfiction by Pam Boyd
Surviving Mother, a novella by Gwen Head
Winter Park, a novel by Graham Guest

About the Poet

With an interest in art, art history, Spanish language studies, and creative writing, Elizabeth Carmer decided to draw from her real-life experiences and international travels to write poetry collections that range from the Iberian peninsula to South America to the steel towns of New England, and travels no less broadly in form, exploring the various, contemporary voices of the poet.

A native of Syracuse, New York, Carmer earned bachelor's degrees in both Art History and Spanish from the University of Vermont, where she spent time abroad honing her language skills and researching for her future writing. After graduating, Carmer began a career in public health, working as an administrative assistant at a community health center in New Hampshire. Having volunteered internationally and locally for community and women's health organizations, including a domestic violence office and Planned Parenthood, as well as a political campaign, Carmer uses her love of writing to harness in her poems a keen eye for culture, politics, place, and the world around her. Her poems are reflective and autobiographical in nature, and outward-facing in thematic scope.

Currently, Carmer spends her time out of work writing and engaging her passion for photography. *Halfway Friends for Decades* is her first work. *They Are Almost Invisible* is her second piece of work.